VERSE VOYAGERS

Edited By Wendy Laws

First published in Great Britain in 2024 by:

Young Writers
Remus House
Coltsfoot Drive
Peterborough
PE2 9BF
Telephone: 01733 890066
Website: www.youngwriters.co.uk

All Rights Reserved
Book Design by Ashley Janson
© Copyright Contributors 2023
Softback ISBN 978-1-83565-330-2

Printed and bound in the UK by BookPrintingUK
Website: www.bookprintinguk.com
YB0577S

FOREWORD

Since 1991, here at Young Writers we have celebrated the awesome power of creative writing, especially in young adults where it can serve as a vital method of expressing their emotions and views about the world around them. In every poem we see the effort and thought that each student published in this book has put into their work and by creating this anthology we hope to encourage them further with the ultimate goal of sparking a life-long love of writing.

Our latest competition for secondary school students, This Is Me: I Am…, challenged young writers to write about themselves, considering what makes them unique and expressing themselves freely and honestly, something which is so important for these young adults to feel confident and listened to. There were no restrictions on style or subject so you will find an anthology brimming with a variety of poetic styles and topics. We hope you find it as absorbing as we have.

We encourage young writers to express themselves and address subjects that matter to them, which sometimes means writing about sensitive or contentious topics. If you have been affected by any issues raised in this book, details on where to find help can be found at www.youngwriters.co.uk/info/other/contact-lines

CONTENTS

Independent Entrants

Nahidul Miah (16)	1
Kadie Davis (16)	2
Sumeiya Jeilani (14)	5
Evie Jackson (18)	6
Andrews Agyekum (16)	11
Abigail Hughes (17)	12
Holly Hopkinson (14)	15
Alexandra Rohvarger (12)	16
Lucy Hewitt (16)	19
Lola Johnson (13)	20
Jessy Otchwemah (14)	23
Sum Yuet (Keisha) Kwok (16)	24
Beatrice Teates (16)	27
Grace Cook (16)	28
Christopher Zaug (15)	31
Anaya Rana (12)	32
Sareena Padayachy (15)	34
Amna Rajput (18)	37
Angelina Simkute (16)	38
Lyla-Grace Thompson (17)	41
Lisa Okrah (16)	42
Aster Carroll (18)	44
Muskan Ditta Afzal (18)	47
Martha Johnson (14)	48
Rameen Ijaz (13)	52
Keira McCann (15)	54
Bernadette Trimmings (15)	56
Thomas Griffiths (15)	58
Jessica Rafferty (16)	60
Yunqi Shan (17)	62
Erin Rose Manning (12)	64
Kiefer David Hewitt (16)	66
Siham Yussuf (15)	68
Caitlin Banfield (16)	70
Victoria Cicha (16)	72
Sienna Thomas (13)	74
Ava Rose Thomas (16)	76
Taya Brown (16)	78
Navah Bialoguski (17)	80
Maria Borowicz (13)	82
Iniyah Khan (14)	84
Nadia Kaczorowska (12)	86
Lewis Godfrey (13)	88
Enara Marinho (12)	90
Holly Hutcheon (16)	92
Kamran Prince Azam (15)	94
Miriam Ajaz (12)	96
Camilla Bailey (16)	98
Amelia Smith (18)	100
Harliv Dhuria (14)	102
Melody Andrew (14)	104
Ava Rice (13)	105
Nishtha Ghelani (12)	106
Luna Rogers (14)	107
Bailey Duncan	108
Syed Nad-E-Ali (14)	109
Beth Lamin (15)	110
Faiha Potrick (15)	112
Mariam Bououne (13)	114
Victoria Allen (15)	115
Samuel Robinson (17)	116
Jessica Leinster	117
Kris Beasley (15)	118
Annabel Quinn (12)	120
Ava Eborall Jackson (12)	121
Peter Zaug (12)	122
Szymon Blasiak (16)	123
Ayesha Afridi (13)	124
Elliot Paton (15)	125

Vishwajanani Vasudevan (12)	126
Tatiana Rose Patterson (13)	128
Laura Orosz (13)	129
Debaroti Choudhury (13)	130
Ayush Guptan (18)	131
Steve Joby (12)	132
Hiba Gillani (16)	133
Megi Gancheva (14)	134
Sona Dukkipati (12)	135
Rose Greiff (13)	136
Avantika Saravanan (12)	138
Isobel Gadsby (12)	139
Adam Seymour (12)	140
Jathurika Thineswaran (12)	141
Nicole De Oliveira Vasconcelos (15)	142
Maja Laskowska (13)	143
Noa Archer (13)	144
Georgina Stafford (11)	145
Owam Makeleni (13)	146
Isabella Marsh (13)	147
Leah Esson (12)	148
Tauheed Ali (17)	149
Miller Webb (12)	150
Harper Nayak (13)	151
Narayan Kolliboyana	152
Saima Khan (11)	153
Alana Bharucha	154
Cleozatra Johnson Watkis (14)	155
Azlan Khalid Noor (11)	156
Nithujen Niranchan (12)	157
Fiona Macmillan (14)	158
Kabiven Vivekanantharajah (11)	159
Emily Schranz (16)	160
Sa'ad Adewunmi (15)	161
Calum Walker	162
Khloe Ndjoli (14)	163
Isabella Nash (13)	164

THE POEMS

DIFFERENT RELAXED FUN LONELY
STRONG FIERCE POSITIVE
OPTIMISTIC ADVENTUROUS
PASSIONATE HAPPY
ANXIOUS

EXTROVERTED STRESSED
FEARLESS AMBITIOUS
LOYAL OK ANGRY
FINE
TOUGH
BORED
MISUNDERSTOOD SAD
GRATEFUL WISE PROUD
CHILL
BRAVE
STRONG KIND INTROVERTED
WISE ENERGETIC
UPBEAT QUIET TRUSTWORTHY

My Future, In My Hands

In a world where dreams take flight, I soar high,
A beacon of happiness, reaching for the sky.
Passionate and determined, with a fire deep within,
A future waits for me, where my journey will begin.

With every step, I chase the light of joy,
Embracing life's wonders, no limits to deploy.
My heart ablaze with dreams, a radiant flame,
In pursuit of justice, I'll leave an eternal name.

As I navigate the path to my desired goal,
Worries may arise, but courage consoles.
Life, a challenge that awaits,
But my dedication and efforts shall seal my fate.

Embracing the excitement that courses through my veins,
Opportunities beckon, a world ready to explore,
With open arms, I'll step through that door.

Equipped with wisdom, I'll leave an imprint grand.
In my passion and perseverance, I truly belong.
Keeping the flame of happiness burning bright,
As I chase my dreams, with all my might.

May my journey be filled with success,
Advocating for justice, making a positive impress.
In this sophisticated yet captivating rhyme,
I celebrate my spirit, my future sublime.

Nahidul Miah (16)

Taken By The Storm

My head is filled to the top with a never-ending storm,
Every thought is the blackest clouds above the middle of the stretching sea.
I was sent out on a boat with no paddles,
Into the bloodshot, numb, teary eye of the storm.
The fog surrounds me with deceiving comfort,
Every powerful wave tries to drag me under,
As my boat slowly sinks I let out some of the water through my eyes,
Enough to just keep the boat floating
but never enough to get to safety.
The cold, red rain drips on my skin,
But I have no blanket to protect me.
The wind gets stronger sometimes,
It is playful like a child that doesn't belong.
Thunder.
That makes my boat rock with fear, lightning.
A false sense of hope in the darkness,
I am lonely, my black and blue boat is my only friend,
Made with memories and happiness carved into its broken wooden figure.
I am trapped by the deep water beneath me,
If I try to escape, the only way is down,
Into the belly of the bloody storm.
But for a minute the surface of the water makes me wonder if the storm will ever pass?

Questions stare back at me from an unclear reflection,
A reflection I have grown to hate but cannot escape.
So I wait here in my dangerously safe home,
For a never-ending storm to finally end.
The waves keep hitting me,
Making it harder and harder to carry on,
But I can't turn back now,
It's too late.
The waves try to drag me under,
But there is an unseen kindness to their nature,
The water whispers wise words,
Words that are the key to shore,
Don't go under
Because there are so many things left to experience on land,
There are thousands of songs from the shells you haven't listened to,
Art beyond the sea you haven't seen,
Movies that haven't changed you,
Lessons on how to sail the sea you haven't learned.
Don't go under
Because there are so many words that haven't been spoken,
People waiting for you to get to the sand,
Little things like sunsets you haven't witnessed,
Different seas you haven't swam in,
Nights that are warm and cosy,
Memories you haven't made.
The water gives me the strength and power when I get tired,

And sends me a message in a bottle to find me when I give up hope of searching,
That reminds me of the love of the land,
The place I call home,
Where there are smiles in the sun,
And hugs of happiness.
The shells sing to me as I get closer to the sand,
The world you see from your boat is cruel,
Because there is a whole other world out of the sea,
And with time you will see it for yourself,
You say you want your world to change,
Maybe it's a world that needs you to change it.
Time is my friend,
It can heal the past and clear the fog,
I have been in this boat so long I became blind,
Distant from shore,
And trapped in an illusion that became my reality,
It made me forget all the wonderful things waiting for me in the future,
When we get there,
It's never too late,
To end what seemed like a never-ending storm.

Kadie Davis (16)

The Realm Of The Unknown

In a world of dreams, I am the song that's never been sung,
In the night my melody is softly strung,
In a universe of widespread words, I'm the unspoken one,
I'm a plate of colours shaded by none.

In a garden of existence, I shine the brightest,
With petals of perseverance, mine was the lightest,
I knew there was always gonna be a twist,
As I finally saw the perfect curdle.

In the realm of the unknown, I am the secret untold,
A riddle wrapped in the dark, a mystery that's stronger than the sharks,
I hide within the whispers of the bright night,
A symphony of secrets that's hidden from clear sight.

Once upon a time, there was a young shy girl,
She had a life that often made her twirl,
Even though she kept her ideas to herself,
Her dreams were stories only time could tell.

Her confidence developed like a fast river,
Soon it turned into a room of shiny silver,
With each challenge, she became the girl she longed to be,
In a world where her dreams were finally free.
AND now this is the new me.

Sumeiya Jeilani (14)

High-Functioning Teen Zombie

Growing up,
Teen zombie always felt the weight of the world
Around her.

Bites at the flesh
never quite healed,
And little teen zombie
felt parts of herself yield.

She wasn't quite sure
when the infection spread.
Nor did she know,
how the bites got so red.

The music had cut out,
Leaving teen zombie
barren to the world's
Thick grey haze.

Her movements slowed,
Her thoughts a fleeting
Trail of fractured segments
Breaking through her memory.

And along with this
birthed a new feeling.
Of nothing,
And of everything all at once.

It was a difficult adaption
at first,
though teen zombie soon
acclimatised to its harsh conditions.

Her brain rewrote into a script of pessimism.

A void had opened,
an anomaly.
Starving little teen zombie
of all the qualities that made her human.

So much so,
She had forgotten to fill this hunger.

So much so,
She missed the world around her.

She found she wasn't present,
and all there was,
was the void calling her back

Calling her back to the eggshells,
she so thoroughly
tried to avoid.

Making her think about
the quote of the bug,
for the crime of being small.

This continued for weeks.
This continued for months.
This continued for years.

It's still continuing.

It's different now,
Teen zombie can
Drift between the
Living and the dead.

Teen zombie,
Learnt to walk the
Line between functioning,
And not.

Though this doesn't make it any less difficult.

But, when little teen zombie
Takes her last steps
out of the void,
she feels the music flood back in.

And she knows,
this is her lifeboat,
keeping her afloat
in her all too-dark mind.

Keeping her afloat,
Until the house feels like home again.

Until she hears her sister
Asking to play hide-and-seek,
To show her the new hiding spot,
She so carefully crafted.

Until her friends make plans to meet,
Until she's getting in the car
with her brother on late nights,
with the music loud
and the speakers booming.

Until she sees her siblings
after a long time away.

Until she wakes up,
With a light heart,
And a steady head.

In these moments,
Teen zombie's heart
Appears to beat.

In rhythm with the music,
taking her
like a tidal wave.

Though soon enough,
Teen zombie can lose her footing,
And the music
Seems to drift.

Taking the high-functioning title away.

Leaving little teen zombie, lost and grey.

Evie Jackson (18)

Earthly Son

I'd say I've encountered some pretty delightful moments in my time,
I've navigated through countless adversaries, awoken on the mountain peak,
I have seen how one man's plantation of a seed is enough to blacken the richness of a soil.
I don't need a crowd telling me what the dream and purposes in this existence should be,
and matter of fact I've never asked anything from anybody.

I am unworthy, undeserving, inexcusable to a legacy that was placed upon me at the unfolding of my creation,
I've never belonged anywhere, never fitted in the shuffling of the crowds,
nobody's son, nobody's daughter.

However, I hold no intent of hatred against anyone in particular.

As the seasons change and the Earth turns I connect with the widespread harmonies of nature's compositions.
With my concluding suspiration I let go of everything around me and finally become what I deserve,
settling down into the warm and moist climate of the soil of the planet I reside in.

While Earth reclaims his earthly son.

Andrews Agyekum (16)

Who Am I?

This is me, I am... I am... I don't know
I look in the mirror and try to find who I am,
to try and find even a speck of something I could be,
and yet I come up empty-handed each time.
The disappointment has started to fade over time
I think or at least I tell myself it has
because that way it's easier to live with the fact
I don't know who I am.
It makes each day spent in the melancholy hue
that has wrapped around me like a weighted blanket easier.
Or at least that's what I tell myself.

I tell myself a lot of things: that I know who I am,
that I am happy,
that each day I am as excited as the last to awake,
that I am content in my life.
I tell myself that I am living
because accepting the fact I am merely surviving,
hanging on by a thread, is a harder pill to swallow.

I pretend that I'm not an anxious person
who is scared of everything,
that even waking up scares me.
I pretend that I'm not built from insecurities and vulnerability,
that my foundations are strong.

I pretend that I'm not unsure about each step I take.
I pretend that I don't need anyone,
that I'm not afraid to be alone.
I pretend that I know who I am.

So maybe I'm the things no one else knows about me.
Maybe I'm the anxiety and sorrow that fills me.
Maybe I am the precariousness and instability that is woven in my soul.
Maybe I am the scars of loneliness that are embedded deep into my skin.
Maybe I'm all the bad but maybe just maybe one day I'll accept the fact that I'm the good as well.
That I'm the selfless girl who puts herself out there to help everyone.
That I'm a kind caring soul who only ever wishes for the people around her to be happy.
I'll accept the fact I have given my all for people who didn't deserve any of me and now it's my turn to experience love, to take and receive instead of always giving.
I'll accept the fact that I deserve good things in life,
that I am more than what others tell me I am.

I'll accept that I deserve this life and I am worthy of love and to be cared for.
That I deserve to be put first for once.
I'll accept that I am good enough.
One day. Maybe... One day I will.

If you ask me who I am I'll tell you I don't know
and that's alright, that's okay.
I am okay.
And that's good enough, this is enough.

I am enough.

Abigail Hughes (17)

Phoenix Rise

My lovely youth, a waste wilderness
With weeping flowers and all grey tones
A youth of everlasting sleep
Sleep by cold firesides in an alienated home
Pondering my dark fate
I lived and inched closer to death as I sang in solitude
Sweet voices and eyes ruined by savage lives
And fond loves wasted into wild eyes
I want to seek strange truths in undiscovered lands
Close loves would have wept to hear my passionate notes of misery

I am a phoenix as I rose up out the ashes of my misery
To reclaim what should have been mine all along.

Make waste of my waste wilderness
My flame will burn every flower and will glow every grey
I became the fire in an alienated home
My dark fate enlightened by a golden flame
I lived. I lived as I sang in solitude
Sweet voices and eyes crackling with a new flame
Wild eyes burned alive to fond love
I found strange truths in undiscovered lands
The truths of loves and freedoms in fields and sands.

Holly Hopkinson (14)

Sometimes I Wondered What I Promised Her

S ometimes I wondered,
O nce, when the dusk slip, slip, slipped along the horizon and the warm
M ay night, when the sparrows fell silent and snuggled solemnly into their nests,
E ver content, and the clouds came to crowd the sky and drip, drip, dripped a river of tears
T hrough the leaves, splashing into a stream,
I nto the hollows and seams of a world too small to see, through the warm
M ay night, mist curling through a forest of daughters of dreams,
E ver courageous,
S ometimes I wondered what I promised my words, my world, my pen to obey me...

I wondered why they meant so much to me.

THIS IS ME: I AM - VERSE VOYAGERS

W hen night has fallen, and chill breaths cut through the air,
O ne star peeped cautiously out from the clouds, then clicked into place.
N ow the sky glinted as if filled with glittering
D iamonds, bobbing along through the sky - an ocean of ink -
E ternally patient. An emerald light shone from a soaring plane, then a thought struck:
R eal stars used to guide sailors, slipping through sea, to safe harbour
E ven then, I knew that words are my stars - they will guide my protagonist, my story-
D eep into a path of colour, of light, to safety.

W hat creatures gaze or glare through closed-off paths, what hesitation
H inders us - tripping, shifting roots and rustling leaves?
A nd thus questions that quench the thirst and courage for answers,
T ick away the time, distract from truth.

I wondered why they meant so much to me - not anymore.

P romises? What promises have I made to a watchful audience,
R eal or fake, random or futile? What have I
O mitted, ominous foreshadowing seeping through the soil of her path?
M aybe misery.
I pause and look up from my desk. It's 1:32am.
S tanding on my bed, I slide the window shut and warm the room.
E ventually, I wonder if I promised her enough, after everything.
D efinitely not.

H ere, I turn off the lights. I nod off, slip, slip, slipping to the beginning of my world of dreams,
E ver afters, once upon a times - to be or not to be?
R evolving, a planet that sparks my world's inferno - my protagonist will carry her story (on her frail shoulders...)

Alexandra Rohvarger (12)

The Battle

To hold the heart that beats for you would be honour enough,
The braveness that it would grant me, to stand when war is tough.
The truth is that I am afraid, not daring like a knight,
I stand upon the battlefield but just observe the fight.
The stories that I've heard of love have been daring and bold,
I fear that mine is not enough to deserve to be told.
Blood does not flow from any gash, none put there by a sword,
It seems I have not done enough to warrant this 'award'.
I cannot march behind the troops, not even hold the flag,
Its body might be weightless but the colours make it drag;
Ashamed and ignominious, not brazen like the sun,
It simply smoulders from within, too little to be won.
So blame the ancient archetypes that I had loved to learn,
For they confined me in this state, with so much more to earn.
Instead, I picture what it's like, just watching from above,
But my body isn't right
to be able to love.

Lucy Hewitt (16)

The Way I Love You

Everything is going to be okay
you told me as you lifted me up like
I was full of helium
the minute my eyes met yours I knew what heaven looked like
You're too broken to be fixed, those words spiralled around in my
head like a tornado
you allowed me to find peace in my own company
trust
trust in my ability
you gave me strength
strength to feel
you take away my pain
I adored you
I hated you
I loved you
I know I'm broken but I hope you can
love me anyway
the way I love you
you allowed me to have control
control over my body, control over my life
you make me, me
once you get in you're never getting.
out

you're like an obsession, an addiction
if life was a book.
you're my favourite chapter
you're water hugging me like arms being wrapped around my
body you're slowly sewing together
the broken pieces of me and giving me hope
hope to heal
I feel the presence of the board
below me as I look out to see the sunken lights on the shore
the tight strap around my ankle giving me security
I've found comfort in your presence
you don't want to rewrite me or change me
you just want to fix me
you bring me back to life
there was always an absence in my heart
like a hole that hole got filled after I met you
you allowed me to love again
love myself again, love other people
the way I love you
the feeling of losing myself felt
like deep sorrow, you're helping me find myself
hear that
that's the sound of sweet intuition
there is an abundance of water surrounding me
splashing me
it takes all the strength and courage

in the world to love yourself
you're giving me the courage
I see the birds above me, able to hear
their flapping wings from the
voiceless surrounding
the adrenaline goes through my body
like intense excitement
I'm the author of my story
you're my muse
I thought I could do this on my own
when in reality
I needed you
you feel like home
I love you more than I love the stars
in the sky or the mountains with the
snowy tips or the comforting sound of a stormy night
I love you more than myself
you are my home.

Lola Johnson (13)

This Is Me

This is me, this is who I am
When I think I can't, my family says I can.
With my eyes filled with dreams and a heart full of fire
I aspire to make the world a place much nicer
It's time to redecorate, this world needs a change,
Love and kindness we must arrange,
Where differences are celebrated, not cast aside,
Where unity and understanding shall forever abide.
Through the maze of darkness, I shall tread,
With Jesus as my guide, and my family as my thread,
I want to break the chains that hold us down,
And build bridges of peace, so smiles can replace frowns
I believe in equality and justice
Not a world which is only full of disgust
No matter colour, age or even gender,
In my heart, there's room for all, to be remembered.
I'll make my voice heard, strong and clear,
To extinguish the flames of hatred and fear,
This is me, this is who I am, just a girl who will always offer a helping hand.

Jessy Otchwemah (14)

Lone Wolf

Bearing my name, a lone wolf howls
in the quiet

before the hundred decisions and indecisions,
she hides from the pressing gazes emitted from
floating heads, drowning with her loping brain

dread, dress, drawling,
droop, drowse, dreaming,
on drags the lone wolf

dying, she saw a generous landscape, wild and
wondrous; she would be adopted by Mother Earth,
whose arms would open solitude for her, her alone

but Earth's cold breath eats at her feet; rodents slip
from her blunt claws; rabbits clucked mockingly;
and she is too weak to climb up the river mouth

and time goes; the pack has gathered in strength,
eyes fixed on high mountains, as they charge
for the prey, the prize, the peak of their tapestry

sometimes they scowl
sometimes they fight to lick the bloody bones;
and sometimes, they leap to claw at comrades" back

she rests her pair of ragged claws on departure
and holds onto the lone wolf's law

but sometimes they crack in sounds like laughter
and whisper strange stories of faith and bondage
carried by their songs of the wind, through

the storm and snow and decaying forests
to the ears of the lone wolf, bound in her soliloquy
in ten miles of silence

and the cry of Death mingles within,
guarding the veil that conceals the Beyond
an abstraction of warm and cold seasons

there will be time...
for the wind to sing a requiem at her funeral pyre -
for her nuzzle to poke at the winter fire - she will be
drawn to the call: she will die. Perhaps she will

reincarnate
as the scientifically accurate lone wolf,
not a projection of fiction, not dreaming

but searching, eyes scanning the Earth's rim
making discoveries, pouncing at every chance
to join Nature's rhyming beat

Resurrection
may not be recognised by witnesses of the pack
may not be fulfilled by the mortal seconds
dependent on the motion of my heart, but

There will be time.

I was a lone wolf; I still am.
I have been unmaking myself alchemically;
I am freeing freedom
from being lovestruck by its shadow.

The lone wolf whistles hello.

Sum Yuet (Keisha) Kwok (16)

As A Child, I Always Wondered...

Why do you choose to scowl,
when the wind hurts himself and lets out a howl?
Why do you let out an exasperated sigh,
when the earth becomes lonely and reaches out for the sky?
For he's only trying to comfort his wife up high,
as she reminisces on their antiquity and lets out a cry.

But with grown eyes.
I wonder less about the sky's cries,
I chose to wonder more about society's lies.

Why do we hush the weeping child,
and accuse them of making a scene over emotions oh so mild?
Why do we leave children alone in the dark,
leaving them afraid of the nameless secrets and expecting them not to leave a mark?
Why do we abandon the tormented and habitues that went amiss,
and simply forget there is an absent conscious floating adrift in a haunted abyss?

One day we'll turn on a bright light,
so our children won't have to wonder deep, into the dark night...

Beatrice Teates (16)

Poet

Do I look like a poet?
Are my eyes alight with searing truth,
Reflecting the world of a cynical romantic
Through glassy green?
Like a poet's.
Do my lips curl with the pressure
Of dwindling words left unsaid,
Trapped metaphors and similes behind teeth clenched in false smiles?
Like a poet's.
Does my skin fit my mind like a glove of flesh,
Woven of stars in absent dark,
Transparency down to the soul?
Like a poet's.
Words, words are weapons
Held to your throat and tearing
Minds, minds are shattered
So take the edged shards and slit it first
Eyes, eyes are blind
Torn out by bloodstained lies and cynical truth
But do I look like a poet?
Or do my hands restlessly shake,
With the lyrical words that threaten
To shatter bone and tear through skin?
Like a neurotic.

Do I look like a poet?
Or is my skin bruised and battered,
Wounds dripping from a broken mind
Onto flesh marred with scars born of desperate release?
Like a cynic's.
Do I look like a poet?
Or are my hands stained with blood,
Eyes distorted by suffering,
Mind bruised by regret,
Lips sealed with self-hatred,
Skin scarred from a broken mind?
Like the girl who is gasping for air,
Suffocated by grief, hatred, terror
As eyes heavy with exhaustion stare blackly at the reflection in familiar silver glass,
Clouded from truth,
Finding shelter in deadly lies.
That girl is a poet,
Dead eyes alight with romanticised cynicism;
Pale lips quivering with words not spoken;
Skin of stars stretched thin over bones, and scarred;
Shaking hands and a body bruised and broken.
That girl is a poet, her poem her body,
Her vessel to despise and destroy,
Her words to remove and alter,
Until there is nothing to remain but sharp-edged shards of a mind that shatters like glass.

Now, do I look like a poet?
Scarred mind unto death,
Hopeful eyes of youth blackened by truth and lies alike,
A girl trapped by silver glass,
And a deafening voice in her mind,
A poet.

Grace Cook (16)

Standing Tall

Onwards they march with pride and power
Through strife, through life, it is their hour
Eyes fall on them as they come into view
The pressure's intense when the world's watching you

For country and for honour
Loss would but bring horror
Victor's name etched in history
The loser's but a mystery.

Imagine the strength of one's legacy
Past striving for the win so desperately
Taxing is the toll taken physically
Elation comes through mentally

Years of preparation come to eighty minutes
And whether the win is by single or double digits
The outcome is still the same
And one single error could be your bane.

Heavy is the head that rules the world
In but four years more people will be hurled
Into more games and a world of hurt
Representing countries with a badge and a shirt.

Christopher Zaug (15)

Presenting... Anaya!

Anaya is my name,
Please let me explain;
When I think of my name, Anaya,
I imagine a luscious papaya.

My religion is Islam,
Let me welcome you with a peaceful 'Salam',
I fast during Ramadan,
In Arabic, I can read the Quran.

At home, I'm learning Punjabi and Urdu,
As a Scottish Asian, I'm good at reciting Burns poems too!
My grandparents live in Pakistan,
They love it when we visit and we always get a tan!

When I look in the mirror, I see caramel-coloured skin,
I'm proud of it but in school, it can be difficult to fit in.
I quite like to stand out,
In school, however, people say things that make me want to shout!
Some people in this world can discriminate,
This is something that I really hate!

There are some things that I truly adore,
They are to read, write, craft and draw,
I am creative and arty,
Yes, I do love a party!

If there is a family celebration,
I always go overboard with, balloons, party bags and decoration!

I love my fun, friendly family,
Together, we all laugh, happily,
If you come over to visit, you will find,
My grandparents in Scotland are extensively kind!

I wear Eastern and Western clothes, both are unique,
I think that both styles of clothes are very chic,
To spice up my bright and colourful clothes, I wear sparkly bangles,
Every time I move, the bangles make a 'jangle'!

I adore travelling and going to new places,
When I think back at the memories, I see joyful faces,
Each time my mum announces a new holiday destination,
For my travel journal, it gives me more inspiration!

When I go to school my brain gobbles up information
I try hard, whether I learn about cells, tech or multiplication,
I'm convinced that when I'm older I'll go to medical school,
Every day I dream of helping patients with professional medical tools!

So now you should hopefully know that I'm Anaya,
A girl with a kind heart and creative energy like a ball of explosive fire!

Anaya Rana (12)

ME (My Empowerment)

Io sono abbastanza,
I am capable of anything and everything
And I am unstoppable,
I break down,
But I also get back up,
I feel the downs,
And I feel highs,
Sometimes I need a good cry,
And I don't even understand why I am crying,
My insecurities define me,
And my perfections change me,
Behind the smile sometimes I am falling apart,
And other times I need to restart,
I am proud of where I have come,
With the limitations and trauma that I have faced,
I am impulsive,
But I have compulsive addictions,
Sometimes it can be hard to breathe,
Because the standards we live up to are extreme,
I am my own sunshine and my rain,
Ink runs through my veins,
And thoughts scatter in my brain,
Sometimes I crash land,
And no one understands,
How I am truly feeling,

I set my limitations,
I overcome my obstacles,
Because I can and I will,
I am who I am,
I am so much more than what people see,
Full of light,
Laughs,
Positivity,
No matter what I can,
If my life was a playlist,
It would be amazing due to all the different genres it would contain,
I stand for love and passion,
And,
I am not a one-in-a-million girl,
I am the once in a lifetime woman because I make the choices I live by in life,
I was bruised and broken from the scars left behind by the previous people who did me wrong,
My circle of friends is small because not everyone belongs on my journey,
I am a little crazy,
Full of magic and chaos,
Love me or not,
Take me or leave me,
I don't pretend to be who I am not,
I am the girl I see in the mirror each time I glance,

Because to me she is the perfect look,
I am still discovering and uncovering me,
My chapters individually don't define me,
But together they create my story,
I am a strong woman because a strong woman raised me
And I can feel safe in my home because I have a loving family,
I know who I am
And who I am gonna be,
But in the end,
Io sono abbastanza,
I am enough.

Sareena Padayachy (15)

Queens And Kings

I sleep off the negative feelings
Because in my dreams, I'm the queen of my kingdom.
I'll be dancing on clouds, ruling with freedom,
My head on the ground for the peace that I needed.
I can do what I want, without a reason.

But the negative feelings draw themselves back
They don't give you a warning, just a knife in the back.
There's no escape from the demons who like to attack
Every inch of your being, because you can't fight back.

But a fantasy world is what I wanna live in.
Because being asleep is much better than living.

But when the sun rises once more
And the rooster likes to roar
Everybody stops their snores
It's time to wake up, face the world.

So you close your eyes and count to three
Because that's how you think of positive things.
Suppressing the bad words and feelings
So that we can all live as queens and kings.

Amna Rajput (18)

Stress

Stress.
Time is ticking, time is of the essence.
Stress.
Squeeze in more hours, this is *your* future.
Stress.
The clock is turning, hours are going, yet I'm in the same place as before.
Stress.
Everything's muddling into one, I've only just begun and I feel I'm not doing enough.
To do:
- Revision
- Revision
- Revision

Yet nothing is going through, and I can't stand this looming pressure that's creeping up my throat, clenching down, taking away my voice, pressing on my back like a weighted blanket too heavy to bear on my own.
Time.
Come on Year 11s your *mocks* are *2 weeks away*
Time.
Focus, GCSEs are soon, you should *not* be fine

TIME!
It's the one thing you cannot buy, I try,
to claw with my hands, to grab tangible time

but it's seeping through, like grabbing some
slime with your hands wide open and it falling
through the gaps
Time,
is running out and I need support or something
of the sort,
I don't know what I want but *I need* this pressure to be
off,
I didn't ask for this nor did I ask for constant changes in my
life.
"Start going to colleges and 6th form open evening"
I wasn't aware I had to do all this on my own,
no warning, thrown into the deep end,
I never learned,
I can't swim,

'But you're not alone'
'Everyone is going through the same thing'

So why does it feel so tragic for me?

I see people going out having fun, while I'm here, at home,
writing and watching and listening to everything *I can*,
doing all sorts of revision techniques that *I can* to *try*
and memorise everything that *I need* for *the best outcome.*

I know, *I pray*, I hope this will all be worth it in the end but I'm struggling to:

- Inhale and
breathe...

Angelina Simkute (16)

This Is Me; I Hate Camping!

My breath drew pictures in the cool icy breeze
As I shuddered in an oversized cocoon.
I quivered in a pool of unwanted rainwater
"Please, oh please just end soon!"

I thought of a warm house with a cosy fire
Where camels and coyotes could survive!
"Oh wouldn't heat and comfort be nice," I desired,
As water would've frozen in my eyes.

As my blistered feet began to boil and bruise
In my barely wearable socks.
I trembled in the pain that I had gained
When I fell on the never-ending rocks.

My back grew knots even Granny's couldn't solve
And my knees were almost arthritic.
I longed for true comfort outside of the tent
As creatures rested alongside it.

As the morning began and I heard crickets chirp
I saw the light of the end of my pain.
As I ripped the zip open, this torment was over!
Me camping? Oh *never* again!

Lyla-Grace Thompson (17)

My Thoughts

Different personalities run through my head,
Picking a different one every morning when I get out of bed,
So many that sometimes I don't recognise myself,
Adopting personalities from the characters in the books on my shelf.
It's supposed to help me feel normal,
Like I fit in everywhere, business, fancy and informal.
I float around friendship groups like a unicorn,
Can't focus on one thing, my head is torn.
I'll stay in on a Friday, Saturday and Sunday night.
Not in a pick-me kind of way but a way where I'm trapped in my fright.
Trapped within the negative thoughts that cloud my mind,
The ones that say I don't belong, that I'm not right.
Why me? I'm always saying,
But then I remember that I've got it easy, what am I playing at.
Calling my life hard when there are wars going on.
Calling my life hard, when people are hiding from bombs.
The ideas that go through my brain,
They drive me up the wall, they make me insane.
I want to stop questioning people's intentions,
I want people to laugh and smile when my name is mentioned.
I want to trust people again,
To stop thinking the whole world is against my peace, my zen.

I hate being sensitive, letting things get to me,
I just want my head to be empty, be free.
From the words that burn my body,
The ones that make me feel inadequate and shoddy.
I want to see myself the way others do,
But then I question if it is bad, terrible, or anything that's not good.
Why am I my worst enemy?
Why am I full of jealousy?
Why am I my biggest hater?
Why am I my biggest traitor?
My everyday questions that I struggle to answer,
Or silly ones like why would you name a star sign cancer?
I hope that when I wake up tomorrow, I'll pick my own personality,
The one I recognise and miss, the one that'll get me back to normality.

Lisa Okrah (16)

A Bear

Inside my den is soft and dry,
I take some time away to cry,
atop my bed of dreams, I lie,
my heart the crest,
and as the outside passes by,
I lay to rest.

But from my coven, I can find,
I haven't left the world behind,
the grinds of life will ever grind,
without my care,
to all of the dead and living kind,
I am not there.

And may their hearts be brimmed with glee,
and never pay a mind to me,
'tis such a dear and costly fee,
for seldom worth,
when I can find myself for free,
such hearty mirth.

The energy that's spent to build,
leaves little surplus for a guild,
no need is there when I am filled,
with fire and passion,
my soul with comfort is instilled,
in tender fashion.

I cannot stop the life I lead,
to coddle every selfish need,
for friendship, kinship, love and creed,
won't keep me warm,
the love that lines my lair can heed,
a winter storm.

These barren walls of empty space,
will fill with anger, grief and grace,
the feelings that I will displace,
although I dread,
I'll keep them safe in gilded vase,
outside my head,

And when I gaze into the Ness,
away the water takes my stress,
as long as I refrain address,
my lonesome state,
it seems I can control the mess,
that pains me great.

My body gives away its power
and from my mind's succumb I cower,
every second, every hour,
a dwindling light,
becoming like the snowdrop flower,
I cede the fight.

A bleak and single wish I save,
that I be left 'lone in my cave,
my problems become small and scathe,
as I must weep,
allow me the recluse I crave,
and let me sleep.

Aster Carroll (18)

The Fantasy And Reality Of Growing

I'm 18, and it doesn't feel right,
Too old to enter Hogwarts, I've outgrown that place,
The Half-blood Camp and Neverland's call,
Seems distant dreams, I've surpassed them all.

I'm 18, I'm not yet seen as fully grown,
Though not a child, a new reality I must now face,
In between the realms of youth and grown-up guise,
Society's complex expectations arise.

I'm 18, nostalgia takes a stronger hold,
Yearning for moments, like Peter Pan, bold,
Hoping to be Percy Jackson, braving each unknown,
And embracing Mulan's courage I've not fully shown.

I'm 18, diving between childhood and adulthood,
Goodbye to the pure illusion, welcome to the crude front view,
Embracing the future steps guiding me away,
Looking back at those moments that sculpted my way.

Muskan Ditta Afzal (18)

More

Who am I? you ask me
Because you want me to fit in a box, neatly
Sealed and labelled like
A character you can shape and bend
To your will. What makes
You happy? What makes you sad?
A list
Of 'likes' and 'dislikes', neatly
Bullet pointed like
A lack of hope, like never
Fighting, never asking, never crying
For 'more!'

Who am I? you ask me
Because boxes are easier,
Sometimes,
For you. Neatly
Tied up with fluttering ribbons to remind you
That they are worth
No more
Than how they are packaged. And
This time
I answer because obeying
- never fighting, never asking, never crying -
Is easier,
Sometimes,

For me. So
I will tell you
A little bit.
But I cannot; will not
Tell you
Everything
Because some of it
Is mine.
And anyway:
Everything
Does not fit in a box.
I am
Loud. But
I can be quiet too.
I am
Opinionated. But
Only because you don't know
What else to call
The truth.
And
I dream.
And
My dreams cannot; will not
Be confined
By you
And yours.
I am

Young, mature, happy, upset, overwhelmed, overjoyed, hysterical, subdued,
Tired.
I am
More.

Who am I? you ask me
Because even if I do not fit in your box, at least you can tell yourself:
"We tried."
And
This time
I do not answer.
Maybe you should have listened
The last time you wanted
To know.
Instead, I think of
What I would say if
I had not been brought up
To hide it.
I am
Loud.
Because I must shout
To be heard. And
To be listened to.
I am
'Opinionated'.
Because I have eyes

And I can see
What is being done
- what has been done -
To this world.
This world that is
My inheritance.
And
I dream
Because I must to survive
In this world.
This world that puts me into boxes and ignores me
When I fight, ask, cry
For 'more!'

Martha Johnson (14)

The Ultimate Victory Is Mine

You may remove any proof of my existence,
With your blinding desire to shine.
You may rub the very losses in my face,
But the ultimate victory is going to be mine.

Does my sickly-sweet smile bother you?
Why are you glowering with misery?
Is it because I walk with such pride,
That has the power to rewrite history.

Just like fire and wind,
With a purpose, I like to think,
I am a fierce storm,
That rises after it sinks.

Did you want to catch me weary?
Sullen eyes with ashen hair,
Never daring to dream,
Never daring to dare.

Does my stubborn nature irritate you?
My contemptible wish to win,
My desire to touch the sky.
Tut, tut, tut, in itself, a magnificent sin.

You may scorch me with your hatred,
You may turn my life upside down,

Why are you struggling to sleep?
Is it because I listen to your ignorance without so much as a frown?

In every pain, every stab, every loss,
The ultimate victory is mine.
From the very beginning of time,
The ultimate victory was mine.

For I am a phoenix, bright and rare,
I am the rosy dawn, the evening air.

I am a meteor, shining like a star in the night sky.
The ultimate victory is going to be mine.
My ancestors were the founders of history.
And one day, their footsteps I shall follow.
The ultimate victory is going to be mine.

With the legacy that my forebears left in my name,
I am a candle, on its fullest, aflame.

The ultimate victory is going to be mine.
The ultimate victory is going to be mine.
The ultimate victory is going to be mine.

Rameen Ijaz (13)

Dealing With Loss

It's been two hours since I lost you.
I had noticed your absence when I got home,
Unpacking had never felt so lonely
Tears pool in my eyes, begging to be let free
And I oblige.

It's been a day since I lost you.
I cry for you, whom I loved so dearly
That night was so lonely without you
Without you, nobody is there to dry my tears
And I cry.

It's been a week since I lost you.
Life moved on, without you
Secretly I knew you wouldn't come back,
Though I would always hope you did
And I wait.

It's been a month since I lost you.
I still cry over you, though I don't think that will ever change
The news of your loss still hasn't sunk in
Nights are hard now, as you aren't there to calm me
And I sleep.

It's been six months since I lost you.
You still cross my mind from time to time
But the pain of losing you also comes back

I suppose a bond like ours could never be broken
And I regret.

It's been two years since I lost you.
I'm moving away from where I lost you
The memories get too much to bear
Unpacking alone since that day had grown familiar
And I leave.

It's been ten years since I lost you.
You don't come to mind anymore
But trust me, I have not forgotten you
The thought of you is so painful I can't stand to remember it
And I change.

I can't remember how long it's been since I lost you.
I can't remember your face,
Or the happiness you once made me feel
But maybe we will meet again soon?
And I forget.

Keira McCann (15)

Quirky

Isn't everybody misunderstood? Misinterpreted?
I have moved from school to school and every single person, every single student doesn't get me.
Yes, I am quirky. Yes, I am unique. Yes, I am different.
But if I am none of those things, what am I?
Am I a robot? A machine?
Or even more of a loner and nobody than I already was?
I try. I constantly try to fit into the niche that all the girls want and fit into too.
But what can I do if I do not reach their standard?
Am I meant to completely change myself?
Change my personality; my looks; my ideals?
Every time I go to school, Monday to Friday, 8am to 3pm,
I hope and pray that somebody will talk to me,
will work with me, will sit with me at lunch.
The funny thing is that even if I make so-called 'friends' they last a few measly weeks.
If I'm lucky it might last a couple of months and a year at best.
The worst and most saddest thing is that these people aren't my pals.
They talk behind my back on their 'secret' group chats, gossiping about me, having sleepovers
and parties without me; calling me names in the corridor, and really making me feel like the fifth wheel;
an outsider who will never be embraced and accepted.

But now I realise how frivolous those wants are.
If people don't like me, don't understand me.
Then that's their problem.
I should be every bit proud of who I am.
I have achievements that none can compete with.
I have a unique identity that none can match.
I am the very best I can be.

So, if you did not know
This is me.

Bernadette Trimmings (15)

Suffering, Strength And Stability

Ups and downs are present everywhere you look in life.
They can be malicious machinations created from the spite of others,
the gracious goodwill of a complete stranger
or even the compassionate comfort of your kin.
At the end of the day however,
whether you've received some form of 'good' or 'bad' - if you aren't content with yourself and what you have outside of those temporary and fragile factors
then what does it matter?
As much as the highs of life can uplift and elevate the soul, the lows can do the very opposite with but the foul flick of their rancorous wrist.

Ask yourself this:
what is it that carefully carves a welcome warmth into your heart's health?
What sadistically slashes and malevolently maims at the solemn scars of those healing wounds? And finally...
what is it that you need to feel as though you'll be content?

I ask this of you because I wish someone asked me these questions before something nefarious happened.

I wish something gave me the truth in a kindly manner with a satisfied smile.
I wish that it wasn't asked by something with such a
grim grin and
gruelling grasp
Something that didn't cancerously constrict around my body whilst mutilating my mind.
Although arduous and hard to accept, sometimes it's necessary.
Through that suffering, I earned a strength I lacked before.
The very power to be
fulfilled with the most minuscule of things in life.
The capability to find peace within myself.
Peace,
finally.
This is me.
I am at peace.

Thomas Griffiths (15)

Who?

In the vast cosmos, a question lingers, "Who?"
Amidst stars and stories, my identity blooms.
Through the pages of life, I seek my cue,
A puzzle of existence, in various rooms.

With each day's journey, I find my path,
An ever-evolving soul, a blend of maths and art.
Through trials and joys, I face the aftermath,
Unveiling the mystery, playing my part.

I traverse the realm of dreams and aspirations,
Where the "Who" becomes a tapestry of desires.
Aspirations weave threads in life's grand foundation,
A symphony of yearnings, igniting countless fires.

In the mirror, I see a reflection, a face,
Yet, beneath the skin, there's an entire world to trace.
The "Who" extends beyond a mere physical space,
Into the realms of the mind, a boundless place.

Through friendships and bonds, I discover more,
The "Who" takes shape in connections we adore.
In laughter, tears, and conversations galore,
Identity flourishes, on these shores I explore.

As I wander through time, and learn from every fall,
I realise the "Who" is ever-changing, standing tall.

In the grand theatre of life, I perform in the hall,
A character with no script, yet giving it my all.

In the grand mosaic of existence, I stand free,
A unique brushstroke on the canvas, as you can see,
This is me, I am, a tale of individuality,
Unfolding in the great epic of humanity.

Through the highs and lows, in joy and strife,
This is me, I am, the sum of all my life,
A character in a story with moments rife,
Scripted by time, amid the world's endless strife.

Jessica Rafferty (16)

My World In A Palm

In the cradle of my hand, a world unfolds;
Five devoted sentinels, their stories untold.
Petite and elliptical nails, a testament true;
Bitten by youth, yet steadfast and true.

I craft symphonies with black and white keys;
Melody dances beneath my nimble fingers.
Beneath my foot, the pedal takes flight;
Tunes echo, filling my ears with their linger.
Vibration beneath fingertips, soothing scent of spruce keys cradles my soul;
Notes intertwine, like day into night.

I fill the canvas with all my imagination;
Spreading colours onto empty spaces
Sprinkle pigments on top
Like baking a cake with tender care.

I breathe shallowly, feel my heartbeat find its pace as my finger lies on the trigger;
A steady aim, a tranquil embrace
A gentle pull, a marksmanship's art
Bullseye! They exclaim, a chorus of cheer.

I knit till dusk's descent,
Yarn gliding through my fingertips

Forming arrays of uniformed knots,
It weaves and expands like dreams in a twirl.

I write,
Words flow on sheets free and endlessly
As ideas burst out like a flood;
Never be wavered by the ink or border of white
For imagination without bounds.

These hands, though small, wield worlds untold,
Chubby fingers, yet their might uncontrolled.
In their grasp, limitless dreams take flight,
For size never dims their radiant light.

Yunqi Shan (17)

A New Chapter

As I watch the new year sevens hesitate at the door,
My mind drifts back to when that was me - just 12 months before,

That morning I was terrified but didn't make a fuss,
I felt genuinely sick with fear as I waited for the bus,

"Have confidence!" Mum reminded me as she'd recently done a lot,
I told her I was feeling fine but she suspected I was not,

At school, I kept on wondering *when is this day going to end?*
Because I still had no idea how I was going to make a friend,

The other girls would curl their hair, do make-up, argue, shout,
And go on social media - which was all they talked about,

But I talked to some classmates who were also all alone,
And ever since, when I'm at school, I'm never on my own,

So as I watch the new year sevens hesitate at the door,
I search the crowd for ones that feel how I had felt before:

Terrified, sick with fear and impatient to go home,
I look around for anyone who is sitting on their own,

And now I see a girl, isolated from the rest,
The others seem to have made friends but she's still looking stressed,

She is just like me but different because she has someone to say,
"It's fine, you will have lots of friends by the end of the day,

That someone is me.

"Hello," I say, "what's your name?"

Erin Rose Manning (12)

Contrast

What a day, let's get to school!
Both you and the weather look awful you fool
I wonder what teachers and work I've got today?
It doesn't matter, you forgot your homework and they'll be hell to pay
Double periods are so tiring, I'm glad it's break...
You can barely complete one task for goodness sake
I have good grades and the proof of it's written down!
You're stupid.

The summer is ending, man I miss June!
The beaming beacon of the sun...
And the shining shingle of the moon...
Never to be interrupted by clouds too soon!
Winter is coming and your heart will turn cold
When plants with petals shining like gold will wither and fold
And brittle structures will endure damp and mould
And to every fireplace, wood must be sold
You and everything will forever be miserable and cold.

Well, guess what?
What?
I'm done with you, and you're gonna be the one who's forgot
For every day and night there is good and bad
No matter the season, cold or hot

Because deep down everyone's an ironclad
But even the strongest ironclads need occasional repair
From those who are special beyond compare
And so for you and me, we must accept our sin
But you must never let the degrading thoughts win
So cherish yourself and embrace your kin
Because history is made by those who can grin!

Kiefer David Hewitt (16)

Replay

The year is slowly closing in on me, as days are turning into minutes, and minutes to seconds.
Anxiety piling up like bricks and countless journeys taking place outside my cosy little box.
I wonder? I wonder? I wonder?

As it repeats.
Sitting on my stiff chair, pondering about all the things I could do, if my world of unrealistic
Dreams suddenly came to life. Over and over again - for what occasion?

Walking home, the never-ending exams leisurely creeping onto my thoughts,
As my eyes are steadily fixated on the weather twisting and turning itself with confusion.

Indulged in the moment, inertia struck me, as everything fell to zero.
Watching the birds race in a straight line in midst of all the chaos,
Leading me down an unfamiliar path.
Made my grey backpack unknowingly reflect my dull mood like a mirror.

Instead of
Waiting to be greeted by the infinite tasks that would devour most of my time.
I would rather enjoy the youth of my endearing teenage life, rather than sitting

Submissively whilst taking the overload of worldly matters, for hours and hours, non-stop.

When I would preferably sleep, sleeping on my soft pillow guiding me towards my irresistible dreams, pulling me like a bar magnet.
However, what's the point?
What's the point when it will all be put on replay like a movie the very next day?

Siham Yussuf (15)

Beneath The Surface

People always tell me that
I'm pretty, I'm amazing and I'm talented
Yet I can never believe them

It's like there's a voice in my head
Repeating, "That's not true,
that's not true, that's not true!"

I'll forever believe I'm not good
enough for other people. That's
why they can't love me, isn't it?

I'm just the other one: the
other sister, the other daughter,
the other friend, the other student.
Always and forever the second choice.

I guess the real question is,
Why should I believe them,
When I'm always put second?

I can't please everyone forever.

As I continue to put myself second
And everyone else first, I begin to
Lose who I am. The person I was
two years ago, who didn't care
what others thought of her.

I am still the football-obsessed,
Concert-loving girl who is happy
And determined to reach her goals,
On the surface!

But underneath the surface,
I am not. It's like a dark cloud swirling
Around my mind masked
By the smile I put on most days.

From now on, when people tell
Me that I'm pretty or I'm amazing

Or that I'm talented I will never
Be able to fully believe them.

Caitlin Banfield (16)

Unspoken Truth

You probably expect a joyful and exciting story,
If this is the case then you are in for a sad awakening.
My name is Victoria and this is me.

I am traumatised, sad, scared.
I went through a lot of dark stuff and now is the time for me to say them aloud.
Monsters are typical in movies, books and TV series,
but I had a lot of them haunting me during my real life.
The shouting. The crying.
I was emotionally abused by a family member.
I remember the neighbours knocking loudly on the door, checking why I was crying.
I pretended to forgive them,
But not after those times. Not after those fights.

I was a victim of online sexual harassment by adult men.
Even today I am petrified because of this.
It is overpowering.

You think the story ends there?
The answer is still no.
I was bullied in real life and online.
By family and strangers.
By children and adults.
By the young and the old.

Where does this story end you ask?
Several suicide attempts.
Even though I don't have them anymore, it still hurts.
I'm learning how to deal with it on my own.
Even if it puts me in a fragile state,
Nothing seems to clear my mind.
I can't forget.

Victoria Cicha (16)

13

In a world that's bold and full of colour,
I'm a 13-year-old soul, a free-spirited wonder,
With my guitar in hand, I strum and smoulder,
In melodies and chords, my stories unfurl and wander.

Skating on streets, I carve my own way,
The pavement beneath, my canvas each day,
I glide through the world with grace and sway,
In the rhythm of wheels, I dance and I play.

With a needle and thread, I mend and I sew,
Creating a tapestry, where my dreams freely flow,
Stitching together a world that I know,
In fabric and threads, my creativity will grow.

Through the lens of my camera, I capture each scene,
The moments of life, where the world's beauty gleams,
Pictures that tell stories, in colours serene,
A world unseen, through my eyes, it beams.

I'm unique, and I'm proud to be me,
With every note played and every new scene,
In the tapestry of life, I'll forever be free,
A 13-year-old soul, embracing all that I dream.

With a guitar, a skateboard, a needle, a lens,
I'll navigate life, my joy knows no ends,

Through art and through love, I'll make amends,
For I'm a young artist, where my heart transcends.

Sienna Thomas (13)

Incendiary

I wish to be a flower.
Sun-drenched and thriving,
reassured by the safety provided
by the thorns at my side,

but I am not a flower.
I'm fragile but
not fragile like a flower,
fragile like a bomb,

with emotions intense and raw,
I'll forever let my heart pour
out into the field
through the roses and the tulips.

The bomb doesn't have to explode
with hatred,
for that isn't the only composition of passion.
It can explode like a firework,
colourful and bright,
like the waves
crashing again and again.
It can explode in whatever form
your heart chooses to pour.

It's both a blessing and a curse
to have a heart so exposed,

it must be worn on a sleeve,
inevitably pricked by the thorns of another rose,

but it's a privilege to love so deeply,
to feel so deeply,
so do so unabashedly,
do so without hesitation.

Flowers and bombs can work as one,
when one explodes,
the other can overcome
the chaos and the noise
that is feared even still.

Let it explode
and speak your truth.
Let the flowers wrap around your ankles.
Let them carry you.

Ava Rose Thomas (16)

This Is Me: I Am Somebody

Why pose a question:
Who am I?
For I truly do not know.
I am a mother's daughter,
A brother's sister,
A lifeline.
I could be a creator,
A maker,
An author.
Yet, that doesn't answer the question.
Beneath the tired war paint
Is a poised face.
A disappointed face chiselled and changed by society,
Confined to an unsteady rhythm
And a modern melody
That forces opinions
For which I truly do not believe.
I am moulded by a society
Of inequality
That is banished and shunned
By truth.
Generation and generation arrive
And yet we are not at peace;
We are at war with inner conflicts
And shamed by the thought we shouldn't think

As we should be grateful
For our position in our world.
So who am I?
I'm a girl chained to stereotypes and false facts.
You cannot tell me who I am
Until the storm of injustice settles
From its mass destruction.
We are all huddled in a lifeboat
Storming away from reality.
In hardships, we stand collectively
Bravely protesting against the waves
Until the air clears and we're home.
Yet, when we are back at shore
We disregard each other,
We aren't kind.
Do not pose a question:
Who am I?
For I truly do not know.
I am trapped in a vicious cycle
And I'm never reborn.

Taya Brown (16)

Alone In Company

How long can she hold them for?
Two creases on either side of her face.
She is floating.
But to her friends at the table,
She is happy and sound,
Only her eyes keep flicking at the revolving glass door.

The world hustled by her,
Around her,
Surrounds her.
A blend of blurs and noise
Her breath echoed in her head,
An empty cave.
Floating.

She is saying something funny,
Reflections in the revolving glass door are laughing,
She catches sight of herself,
An expression plastered onto her cheeks,
Creases shape around her mouth,
Her eyes,
Cracks in her make-up,
Cracks of a smile.

Tears hid behind her eyelids,
Like a cloth holding back a tsunami;
A silence as waters retreat,

All seems fine at shore,
No one saw
The warning signs,
No one else saw what she saw
In the revolving glass door.

She felt the walls shaking,
Felt the cloth breaking,
Felt that storm that was brewing
Come into the making,
Felt her lip wobbling,
Felt the rain leaking
Through the cracks in her face,
That smile pretending
She was in a safe place.

Navah Bialoguski (17)

Square Nature

Hands
My definition. Like the soul
Seeping into the world through open palms
My hands
My weakness. The point where the barrier breaks
Like waterways weaving the great reefs
And flooding pages with ink
Pages of secrets and reminiscences galore
And my hands
Where they droop
Twitching with the pulse of my veins: trees
Rooting up my skin with staining iceberg pigments
Almost muscly but still knobby, pallid to the bone
But thick to the thumb
Channels of graphite are my bruises
My bruises are my blood
But blood clots and sweat dries
Scars are adorned with steel rings
Of thornless roses with luscious leaves
To let them keep pity for themselves
Although nothing can truly mask
My dumbbell callouses and contorted finger joints
I won't wear gloves but more sports tape at dusk
And rupture the chains from my pockets, let my palms point
And outline the growing swirls of the journey

And one day
These strong hands
My hands
Will lift me from the swathe of memories and daydreams
And plant me in the presence
Of any precious moment.

Maria Borowicz (13)

It's A Need Not A Want

I want to cry
I want to scream
I want the tears to wash all this pain away
But I can't

I want to cry
I want to scream
I want to not feel the emotions I feel
But I can't

I want to cry
I want to wash out everything
But my eyes do not allow tears to fall

I want to cry
Because my heart hurts so much
Because my chest aches more than possible
More than I can imagine
But my tears are denying me the pleasure of washing my pain away

My eyes are against me once again
I don't know how to not feel like this
I don't know how to transfer the inner pain elsewhere

I want to cry
I want to scream
But I can't

So instead I abuse the walls with my fists
Instead, I harm myself using the power I have been given wrongly
Instead, I cause pain to my hands until they bleed
So they can cry away the emotions I feel
So the blood becomes my tears
So my eyes do not need to cry

But still
I want to cry
I want to scream
I want the tears to wash all this pain away
But I can't.

Iniyah Khan (14)

This Is Me

I listen to the dark voices in my head,
I listen to all the things they have said,
I can't escape,
I have fallen into a trap.

Don't listen to them I tell myself,
You are better than them my loved ones say,
Keep going my coaches tell me,
And so I do just that.

So this is me,
Standing here,
Going far
To follow that passion,
That I am keen to have.

I stand up high,
Take your marks,
I crouch down low,
Go,
I dive straight in.

I kick my legs and swing my arms,
I don't look side to side,
I sprint and I swim,
Come on,

It's the last length,
You can do it!

I touch the wall,
Look at me,
I can do it,
And I have done it.

Look at me,
Don't see the me I pretend to be,
Don't hear the ugly voices
See the real me.

And here I am,
Standing in the top 10,
Proud of who I am,
Knowing there are still lots more passions to find.
I am me, this is me.
This is me! This is me! This is me!

Nadia Kaczorowska (12)

Techie

I am a teenage techie boy
I like to play games all day
When it comes to coding
I blow others away

Among my other interests
I also like to cook
I know it's not normal for boys but
I have some recipe books

The internet has lots of recipes
And I mostly get them from there
I don't download all of them
Especially if there is a pear

When we go on holiday
I like to take a boat and sail
Whenever I'm out on the sea
Unfortunately, I don't see a whale

If only when I'm sailing
I could wear a headset of VR
Then I'd be able to see a whale
It would seem like it's not far

On a cold holiday
I also like to ski

No matter where I am
I can even do it in the sea

There are places you can go to
Where machines make giant waves
They also make quite small ones
But the biggest are my faves

If anyone needs help with tech
Call me 'the techie boy'
Don't go playing with it
Because it's not a toy

Lewis Godfrey (13)

Who Am I?

Me, who am I?
I am a fun and creative person

I love to sing and dance
Fling my arms around and prance

I love to dress up in the latest fashion
But reading is certainly my passion

It's amazing to lose yourself in the pages of a story
I do like one such as 'Finding Dory'

A little reading could be perfect for me
If I have my nose in a book, get ready to stand there and plea
I can be silly at times but only to get what's best for me

I love playing games, whether they are board games or not
I will never leave Monopoly to rot

I love to paint and sketch
Though in my eyes, I am not very good yet

I run around all evening long
Yet I am still awake while time has gone

A good movie for me is Nanny McPhee
But my favourite, Matilda will always be

Arts and crafts? A resounding, "Yes please!"
Something I have always been good at is writing one of these

I love a good poem, story or theme, that is all from me,
This is me.

Enara Marinho (12)

The Omniscient Bystander

It is said, that if one door closes
Another opens
To deliver us to a brighter future.
It is also said that the grass is greener
On the other side
But I don't want to move.
I stand on the threshold
Just one of the flock, waiting for their leader.
Just one step. One step closer.
And I will be on my way.
To bring myself to a brighter future.
Yet we'd all rather wait here, for someone else to take the reins.
The door is closed, and we have the key.
But we choose not to unlock it.
I now know why
We have shut another door to block out the bitter cold.
We are afraid.
Afraid that this path will bite us too.
I am not a risk taker.
We prefer to glance through the window.
Watch others lead the lives we were promised.
Standing on the threshold, I can feel the summer sun.
See others on the path to greatness.
One path of many.

Truly, I say, I am happy with my lot.
Except I'll never know if it's better than what I could have got.

Holly Hutcheon (16)

The Future

We are all going to die...
Either we kill each other or
the world will kill us,
Like an *infection*...
Was it our fault?

Live news distracts us from the millions of graves built up by war,
A robbery,
A car crash,
A murder.
Yet, no *genocide* of millions of young people,
All *indoctrinated* with ideas of patriotism or hope,
Yet to die like the rest of us.
Was it our fault?

No trees.
Only one in the middle of a street
surrounded by a metal fence entrapping it,
The rest of its family has been *slaughtered* by us
used to create the paper for our own distractions,
Was it our fault?

More people around me, just shells of themselves
No vibrant nature,
No happy couples,
No one is happy here,

Only the *brainwashed* people, dumped here to walk the streets
as our humanity is lost, for the illusion of gain.
Was it all our fault?

Kamran Prince Azam (15)

Peer Pressure

I tread,
With unsteady footsteps
Little by little.
I weave my way, through the unknown.
Awaiting the challenges
Embracing the wins.
When I come across the high school hurdle
Or begin something new:
A club or a team
I tell myself to be myself,
Yet I always end up not being me.
Trends after trends,
Come in the way.
Of my already busy day.
I should have spent that hour on homework,
But instead, I spent it scrolling.
Scrolling, scrolling.
Through endless nonsense
A waste of time.
Stop! I tell myself.
But it's too late.
It's already ordered.
A waste of money
I'm already tired.
But others think differently.

"Let's go shopping!"
A waste of energy.
But when it all starts building up.
It's best to take a break from hiding
A break from being self-conscious,
And take the next step
Your
Own
Way.

Miriam Ajaz (12)

The Routine Lamentations

Grief acts as a childhood home -
the familiar embrace of an old companion
welcomes your salt-stained skin

in misery, you can watch it all pass by.
waves of classmates, fleeting lovers, passing strangers
you're removed in your refuge
fortified by years of what-ifs

sorrow is a soft cocoon.
beckoning you into its warm caress
the routine smiles,
unconvincing "I'm just tired's"

fear is a safety line.
worried glances, hushed conversations
yet after a few months they disappear,
return to the harsh light of day

they loosen their grip
on your rigid limbs
you can't save someone
who doesn't want to be saved

sit, lay, burrow
wallow in the desperation
the crushing weight of happiness
grounds me in my lamentations

it's unfathomable
the thought of anyone
wanting to save you.

Camilla Bailey (16)

Anxiety

I feel you here
I know you're near
What do you want? I ask
I'm trying to complete my task
Thoughts racing, hands shaking
I can't do this anymore
Your voice, it leaves me sore
I fall to my knees
Begging, leave me, please!
Breathing deeply to no avail
Heart-aching, feeling worthless
Hoping, praying, nothing less
Leave, leave, you cause me so much pain
It's driving me insane
Pressure, pressure is what I feel
I wonder, I wonder what is real?
How should I feel? Could I heal?
Take away this pain that I constantly feel
You take my breath away
And linger every day
I know what you're called, I know your name
I'm ready if you want to play this game
Your name is Anxiety and I'm ready to fight
Fight off the pain and help me feel alright

You don't and won't control me
It's time you leave me be.

Amelia Smith (18)

Who Am I?

I'm not a stranger to the dark,
Not an enemy to the light.
Not hiding in the shadows,
But not in the spotlight.

Some days I look in the mirror,
And I love what I see.
Other days I look too closely,
And wonder, who is she?

Make-up covers my flaws,
A smile hides my pain.
What's the point of acting nice?
There is nothing I will gain.

But this is who I am,
Perfect or not.
This is who I am.

My face shines with make-up,
A smile brightens my day.
Head up high, I know my worth,
Confidently leading the way.

There are days I look in the mirror,
And I love what I see.
Other days I look properly,
And I know, this is me.

I'm not a stranger to the dark,
Not an enemy to the light.
Not hiding in the shadows,
But now in the spotlight.

Who am I?
I am me.

Harliv Dhuria (14)

My Love Is Me

My love for you will stay the same,
It doesn't fade or get dull with age,
You're the one I admire,
You're the fire, the one filling me with desire,
I know your love will never be mine,
But despite knowing you'll never love me I'll still be fine, that's why,
That's why when I look upon the mirror I say these words to myself,
Knowing that's the soul my parents love, not the façade at school when I'm somebody else,
She's different in beautiful ways, the way she styles her hair, the way it flicks and sways,
Her voice far from numb, it was hard to look away as the melodic notes left her mouth in a lovely hum.
She looks back at me,
My brain crushed as her smile began to fade,
She'd realised what they did to me,
Tried to change me into something I didn't want to be.

Melody Andrew (14)

This Is Me

Within my heart, emotions swell,
A sea of feelings, ebb and swell.
In joy and sorrow, I'm set free,
This is me, a whirlwind sea.

A canvas painted with love and strife,
Emotions sculpt the landscape of life.
I embrace each tear and every smile,
This is me, a mosaic worthwhile.

In a world that's quick to judge and stare,
I learned to love the body I wear.
With curves and edges, strong and free,
This is me, in body and soul unity.

For beauty blooms in diverse forms,
In every shape and skin that adorns.
I find strength in self-acceptance's plea,
This is me, in body image harmony.

Embrace the heart and the mirror's view,
For in your essence, a world that's true.
Through every feeling and every decree,
This is me, a blend of emotions and body.

Ava Rice (13)

This Is Me: I Am...

This girl lives in a paradoxical environment.
She is bold, but she hides like a whisper in the throng.
A spirit that is paradoxical - both icy and fiery -
Let me tell you the story of her good and bad traits.

She will speak her thoughts and boldly declare what others
leave behind with unfettered confidence.
However, the shade that darkens her eyes is bashful.
Alone with her thoughts, a peaceful labyrinth.

She is a truth-teller, and although quiet is her armour
a shield she cannot afford
She uses words like a weapon.
Even though she has an unceasing flow of honesty, she
struggles to pursue her own goals.

Sometimes rude, her candour might offend,
She is a devoted friend, yet at her heart, she is kind.
You can come into a conundrum of paradoxes,
In her soul, benevolence intertwined.

Nishtha Ghelani (12)

Too Little

I care too little
I never do
It kinda felt a little different when I met you
My heart started pumping louder each time
And for a moment
It felt like maybe I didn't care too little this time
I swear it was a one-time thing - I don't care anymore
But at that moment, I think I cared too much
Way too much
More than before.
I held on to the note you gave
All ripped in my hand
Did I actually care about the imprint on my hand?
The only thing left to read was 'I love you more'
Ouch, it felt like an eyesore
The words I never thought I'd say
"I love you too"
But it's too late
I throw it away
Too far to reach
No one else to hear this speech
To say I cared too little would be a stretch
Because I cared too much
I think this fits best.

Luna Rogers (14)

Football Poem

The game of football is oh so great,
I enjoy playing it with my mates,
I shoot and score and run on the field,
Tempers flare, I do not yield.

I play in all weathers day and night
In assorted colours that are so bright.
The players run with all their speed.
And I do my best to take the lead.

The manager shouts to shoot the ball,
I go off to score but sometimes fall,
All the players and coaches laugh with joy,
I carry on without a fuss, oh boy.

When the weather is sometimes rubbish.
It can make the pitch really sluggish.
The fans all cheer, shout, and scream
As the players chase their wildest dreams

The game is done, the players are proud.
We celebrate a win really loud,
We shake the hands of the other team
We give our strips to mums to clean.

Bailey Duncan

Happiness

Life treats me well.
Thoughts sound in my head like a bell.
Keeping my true emotions in a cell.
Always hiding inside my shell.
Started to dwell.
Being attacked like a white blood cell.
School attached to my brain cells.
Emotions taking flow like caramel.
Always get knocks on my doorbell.
My strange feelings started to befell.
Didn't know who to tell.
I knew I had to rebel.
Then, felt magical like a spell.
Happiness I could smell.
Joy exploded my feelings like a bombshell.
Heavy weight lifted off my shoulder like a dumbbell.
Still learning organelle and chlorophyll.
But flowed to the top like a gel.
Thought I would get expelled.
Started to excel.
Went from being trapped in a jail cell, to happiness flowing through my nerve cells.

Syed Nad-E-Ali (14)

The Seven Monster Emotions

I am Happy,
A round, yellow monster,
All smiles and angelic,
Greeting everyone with warmth.

I am Sad,
A blue droplet,
A frown upon my face,
The clouds inside begin to rain.

I am Excited,
A fuzzy ball of energy,
Whose rays of light explode,
A burst of happy colours that bounce around the room.

I am Angry,
A fire burning bright,
Flames inside me ignite,
An unstoppable wave of emotion.

I am Shy,
A timid little monster,
All curled up in a ball,
Who rolls around and hides in the corner.

I am Worried,
A curved and shaking wreck,

Who always fears the worst,
Who quivers when nervous.

I am Hope,
A bright and radiant light,
A candle that never wavers,
A flame that never flickers.

I am Me,
A bubbling potion of emotion,
A swirling sea of how I feel,
The person I am meant to be.

Beth Lamin (15)

I Am...

I am...

I will never be a poem,
Perfectly crafted and sculpted,
Each word flowing onto the next,
A utopia of coherence.

My mind is not a haven,
No clear start or end to the madness,
A tangle of thoughts and memories,
Colliding together.

I have never been the greatest,
Not the funniest of my friends,
Good grades but never the best.

In a world of superlatives,
They say to be on top,
As if ordinary was a crime fit for the weak.

My head,
A prison of my own making.
My heart,
Shattered and out for the taking,
Scattered across the pages,
In the notes of my favourite songs,
And words of my favourite characters.

I will never be a poem,
My flaws shine like the night.
I am not a piece of art.
I am messy and unpredictable.
I am what I love,
And what I love,
I write.

Faiha Potrick (15)

Monster

I don't know what to feel,
my head has been acting like the Belfast Confetti,
or a mixture of feelings for a cake or a pie,
I don't know what's wrong with me,
Who am I? What am I?
My head feels like a mix of laugh and cry,
I just want to die.
I'm wanting to seek help,
but no one hears my yelps,
my head acts like a helicopter,
because what follows me is a monster.
A monster who is invisible to the human eye,
but I spy, with my little eye,
a monster that will creep till I die.
I want to seek help but my voice is too low,
which makes time a lot slower.
Who am I?
What am I?
That monster will not creep till the day I die.
Is there really a monster behind me,
or is my insanity getting the better of me?
They just don't understand,
When will be the day I get to stand?

Mariam Bououne (13)

There But Not There

To exist without consequence is a comforting fantasy,
an endless loop of nothingness
consuming every aspect of your being.
To only observe the life of others without any confrontation,
free from the heavy burden of a self
and the responsibilities of humanity.
To disappear into an entity without emotion,
and experience only the peace of being alone.
This, however, is nothing but a delusion.
Completely out of reach, an improbable reality
my brain has manufactured to give me self-assurance.
Something that resembles my feelings in everyday life,
yet, is not actuality.
It's an empty feeling, not to say that it's a bad or good one,
it's just there.
Like myself; just there.
But my mind is elsewhere.

Victoria Allen (15)

Next Year, Where Will I Stand?

Next year, where will I stand?
Every choice ripples forward,
What once was abnormal
Now presents itself as routine,

Every choice ripples forward,
The outcome of indecision
Now presents itself as routine,
Moments missed yet new ones made

The outcome of indecision
Fictitious possibilities turn the tides,
Moments missed yet new ones made
What could become, lost to overthought,

Fictitious possibilities turn the tides,
Seen composure hides anxiety,
What could become, lost to overthought,
Branching predictions, too many to count,

Seen composure hides anxiety,
A single option weighs the soul,
Branching predictions, too many to count,
Next year, where will I stand?

Samuel Robinson (17)

My Older Sister

I can't believe that my older sister never had an older sister,
who was there to teach her how to do make-up
or alert her when our mum was mad,
who was there to give fashion advice
or comfort her when she was sad.
Whenever I cry she is always there
and whenever I'm stressed she will always care.
We have grown to the age that we like to share,
we like to gossip and we like to compare.
I copy her music taste, I copy her style
and I love going down the streets of Argyle.
My older sister is my favourite person,
she inspires me greatly and should never feel like a burden.
I could not imagine life if I did not have her by my side,
I can't believe my older sister never had an older sister.

Jessica Leinster

The Dress

The dress:
Elegant and unmissable
but yet,
Unwearable!

Everyone said, "Wear it,
it's beautiful"

I said, "No
That's not who I am"

Everyone said, "Wear it
it's just a dress,
don't be so dramatic"

Everyone says, "Wear it
it's who you should be"

I say, "No
This isn't who I am"

They're still persistent.
The dictators of a life I can't call my own.

They said,
"Live your life"

They said,
"Be who you are
unless you don't fall in line"

They warned.

This was never about that stupid dress...

Kris Beasley (15)

Who I Am

Why should I care what you say?
I care who I am, and that's okay
You try to beat me down, make me sad
That's just vile, that's just bad

I try to be fierce, happy, alive
But I'm just annoyed by period five
You call me names, try to upset me
But I know that my friends all disagree

Yes I do have friends, though you might think not
And they are all really kind, the whole lot
They don't bully, they're not mean
No, they're always really supportive on that type of scene

Yes, that's who I am, happy and brave
And maybe you shall be forgiven
Possibly, maybe, I'll make my decision
And know who I am with great real precision

Annabel Quinn (12)

My Opinions

I woke up in the morning
Thinking about what the world could be,
without arguments, politics and more.
How simple life could be,
If only we could wake up and see.

If there were no more wars,
Only kindness and peace,
The world would live in happiness
Forever and more...

If only people could see how young people like me,
Could view the world,
Different shapes and sizes,
Love and hate,
If only people could see how delightful the world could be.

When people are in their pyjamas, watching TV,
Not even thinking about life itself,
Not even dreaming about what it could be,
People only have one life,
They may as well live it...

Ava Eborall Jackson (12)

The Stream Of Life

Down the valley, the stream goes
It goes to the ocean, where it comes from unknown
The stream of secrecy
The stream of honesty
The stream of democracy and theocracy
Gushing down, filling up
Is it poisonous? Is it dead? Are there creatures inside? We shall see
The stream of death
The stream of life
The stream of chance and fate
It all is a leap of faith
Seas heating down. stream hurrying up
Global warming, hey! What's up
The stream of coming times
The stream of past ones too
The stream of joy
The stream of anguish
The stream has passed us now
So we live on, through our boring lives
Waiting for another stream to come by.

Peter Zaug (12)

An Environmental Sonnet For The Blamed

Many claim we are ignorant
Interestingly this is hypocrisy,
Somewhere the economy needs an invigorant
Unfortunately, the truth is that you only care about bureaucracy.

Nasty, notorious, nefarious corporations pump sewage into the water
Doing so they give you lucre,
Environments are in anguish in this process of biological slaughter
Really you are the ones who truly need a tutor.

Such buffoons are in power
Thanks to their negligence we get the blame,
As a matter of fact, we are the foundations of this tower
Now is the time for us to exclaim!

Destroying our future is a crime
So quit blaming us and for our planet please spare a dime.

Szymon Blasiak (16)

Broken

Every day, every night
Life seems lost
Out of sight

A few to trust, a single tear
I don't know about you but
Can you smell the fear?

Yes, I am afraid
Of this vile world.
With oceans so deep and stories to be heard.

I have yet to explore this world of nature
That not all people savour.

You may see me as daring
But once you get to know me
I am most caring.

Yet my smiling eyes do cry tears
And so, may yours
Let us cry quietly so no one hears our sorrows

I want to be there to wipe away your tears
And just like that, you might forget your fears

Roses are red, violets are blue
Our lives have been broken
But we fix them with glue.

Ayesha Afridi (13)

I Think Maybe Sometimes

I think maybe sometimes I want to die
I think maybe sometimes the feeling is so strong it makes me hold my breath
I think maybe sometimes there is a creature curling its talons around my oesophagus squeezing till I pass out
I think maybe sometimes I am not in control
I think maybe sometimes I don't want to die
I think maybe sometimes the creature is thinking for me, sinking his teeth into my brain, tying string to my limbs
I think maybe sometimes he is in control, contorting my limp body until it does what he pleases
I think sometimes I am a puppet, a rag doll
I think maybe sometimes there is no creature, it is just me in my head and I am in control.

Elliot Paton (15)

Totally Ordinary Yet Totally Extraordinary

This is me.
My head flooding with thoughts,
My heart bleeding with emotions,
Oozing with an iridescent colour of emotion,
I am happy yet sad,
I am scared yet still brave,
I am angry yet still content,
This is me.
With caring and amusing parents,
With an annoying sibling,
With marvellous friends and irritating enemies,
With an imagination to immerse myself into,
This is me with my own unique beat to dance to,
This is me with a whole life to wake up to,
This is me.
Understanding, passionate, enthusiastic,
Envious, dramatic, sensitive.
A kaleidoscope of emotions slowly shattering,
This is me.
Totally ordinary and totally extraordinary,
In every way.
I am myself, me and I.

This.
Is.
Me.

Vishwajanani Vasudevan (12)

I Am Fabuloso

I know how the sun dies,
I know how bullies destroy hearts,
I know why people have different feelings,
I know how love heals a broken heart,
I know how clouds burst,
I know why tears are salty,
I know why sadness is blue,
I know why the sun smiles.

I have been a dove trying to find peace,
I have been a field of flowers trying to escape the crowd,
I have been a crying cloud,
I have been a laughing ray of sunshine,
I have been a cygnet coming into my own,
I have been a tornado creating chaos,
I have been an eagle watching over,
I have been an angel,
I have been the devil,

I am fabuloso.

Tatiana Rose Patterson (13)

What If I Am?

What if I am?
Some call me kind and caring,
Always thinking about everyone,
Making people happy even if I suffer,
I know it's not healthy being that someone.

What if I be?
Some call me geeky and weird,
Always being the silent wallflower,
Being fluent in languages yet refuses to speak.
They call me a witch like I have a superpower.

What if I do?
Some call me sporty and fighter,
Always swooping perfectly like a peregrine,
Ready to catch the sweet taste of victory.
At any given time, my talons shall be seen.

What if I shall?
Fellow person, have you ever wondered
What if I am?

Laura Orosz (13)

Who Am I?

I often wonder who I am,
A canvas of many dreams and hopes
A collection of highs and lows
But who am I? Who can I trust?
In the maze of life, which direction is just?

Searching around for clues,
What have I got to lose?
Everything's corrupted and so is the news,
What's the point in telling lies?

Confused, realising that everyone had left,
Trying to comprehend. Is this a threat?
Or is it a theft?
What is happening?

Ringing sounds in my head,
Similar to the squeaky sounds in the old shed,
I looked around and fled.
Out of my home, out of the city.

Helpless, I cried,
I searched everywhere, teary-eyed.
Hoping to find her by the seaside,
Who am I? And why am I here?

Debaroti Choudhury (13)

Boarding School

I stare aimlessly at my cellular
With every scroll a dopamine hit
To distract myself completely
From this feeling, I cannot omit

My friends back home post repeatedly
It hurts when I am stuck in this condition
Their pictures each tell a story, sing a different song
Yet I am sick of these renditions

I simply cannot articulate
My lonely sentiment
7,000 miles from home
The distance feels so evident

Maybe one day I shall look back
With a smile and say,
"Thank god for that school; I learned so much."
However, unfortunately, that day is not today.

Ayush Guptan (18)

Just A Nice Guy

I like the feeling of not knowing what a new day will bring,
But I also like choosing my future.
What will 2070 be like?
Will AI dominate the world,
Or will humans deprive Earth of its resources?

There is no excuse for not trying to learn,
My future relies upon my decisions.
Success is only an arm's reach away,
It is only a matter if I can grasp it or not.

I saw a person struggling to learn.
I encouraged him to not give up, to not let go of his dreams.
I helped him get closer to his goals and gave him the determination to reach there.
I am just a nice guy.

Steve Joby (12)

I Love Who I Am

I love who I am
What is the point in struggling to fit in
When we were born to stand out?
We should not allow what other people expect of us
To shape who we are
If we allow others to have so much control upon our life
Is it really our life?
8 billion people in the world and we are all different
None of us are the same
Because we were born to stand out
In a crowd of 8 billion people
What makes you, you?
Your humour, loyalty, maybe your selflessness
Don't let anyone tell you to change yourself
Or to stop being different
Because we should love who we are.

Hiba Gillani (16)

Reflection

Every single morning,
I am asking my mirror.
"Is my life warm like the spring,
Or is it freezing and lonely like the winter?"

Every single afternoon,
I have to pretend that I am fine.
Hiding my insecurity with the smell of expensive perfume,
I dream about the day I can finally shine.

Every single night,
I realise that there is nothing wrong with me.
I can be myself only when I am illuminated by the moonlight
Because only the darkness makes me feel free.

Every single day,
I repeat this again and again.
However, I still love being myself
Because I am the one who I will never betray.

Megi Gancheva (14)

My Life

I'm like a puzzle, but also a book
I don't make sense, but you'll want a second look!
I love to dream, but I'm grounded too
I travel around, but I know where to go!

I love life, even when it's tough
I'll fight my battles, that's not a bluff!
I'll listen to you, and care with my heart
I'll take in the world and stay sharp and smart!

I create things, what's in my head
I believe in words that need to be said!
I'm just myself, with my own special flair
I'm here for a while, so let's have some fun and share!

Sona Dukkipati (12)

Be Proud

Burnt, dark orange, like
Autumn and fire, gender
Non-conformity.

Strong, bright orange, like
Clementines and marigolds,
Independence.

Pale, light orange, like
Peaches and sunstones,
Community.

Pure, cool white, like
Bones and snowfall, unique
Relationships to womanhood.

Gentle, impactful pink, like
Cherry blossoms and axolotls,
Serenity and peace.

Soft, dusty pink, like
Roses and dusky velvet,
Love and relations.

Bold, dark pink, like
Raspberries and lotus flowers,
Femininity

Suns set and suns rise
But the flag will never waver.
Be proud!

Rose Greiff (13)

This Is Me: I Am

Everyone has their own identity,
Something to go by, something they're known as,
Is it their smile, special eternally?
Or maybe their eyes, glinting like topaz.

Some people are talented and gifted,
With tricks and gifts, skills and secrets to share,
The community's spirits are lifted,
Smiles on our faces, expressions of care.

But sometimes, it's a little bit deeper,
When people are scorned for their uniqueness,
Race, age or gender, who's superior?
Embrace each other, fighting is pointless.

This is me; I am a warrior too,
When we unite, freedom has no taboo.

Avantika Saravanan (12)

Proud To Be Me

I have freckled pale skin
And a whitish toothy grin
As well as thick brown hair
And a beady green-eyed stare
I want to go to Oxford to study law
Or be a world-famous activist on tour
I would love to play badminton for Leicestershire
Or hold a spider without any fear
I want to play viola in an orchestra so grand
Or maybe just in a simple garage band
And I know in life that I will fail
But I still want to tell my tale
A tale of joy, love and happiness
But also, a tale of hardship and sadness
Because this is me
And I am proud to be me.

Isobel Gadsby (12)

This Is Me

This is me
Through my highs and lows
And my ups and downs

This is me
Through my struggles and achievements
And my failures and successes

This is me
Through my mum and my dad
And my brother and my grandma

This is me
Through my family and my friends
And my ancestors and my mates

This is me
Through family walks and adventures
And hikes and climbs

This is me
Through my beliefs and my opinions
And my ideas and my views

This is me
Through my past and present
And now my future

This is me.

Adam Seymour (12)

Difference

Here on a planet called Dupiter, I live here.
Everyone has five eyes but I have four eyes.
Why was I born like this?
Looking up at the sky,
I admire the green and blue masterpiece called Earth.
I've heard about humans in stories.
However, I do not know if it's true.
I'm a creature that has wide pointed horns tipped with brown, and glowing hazel eyes.
Two yellowing canines overhang my red lip.
I have five fingers on each hand so that means fifteen fingers altogether but my friends have ten fingers.
Why am I the only one like this?

Jathurika Thineswaran (12)

This Is Me

This is me,
a mosaic of emotion
love with endless devotion,
I am a body in constant motion.

I am the rain,
for I dance with no shame.
With glistening eyes which for a moment, hold no pain.

Do you know my name?
When I ask, your answer, it's the same.
I know no restraint
I do not wish to fit in your frame.

I will not take the blame
all because you've chosen to peruse fame.
Throwing insults like it's a silly game
Do you know my name?
Because when I ask, your answer, it's the same.

Nicole De Oliveira Vasconcelos (15)

Ode To The Ardent Dancer

My mind is an explosion
of enthusiastic fireworks,
when I step out on stage.
The lights are glowing and glittering,
glistening and glimmering.
The audience,
hopeful and eager,
prepared for a spectacle.

Some days I glide like a falcon
and soar up and down the room,
but other days I'm just polishing
my tendus, or fighting to keep up my leg
"Just 8 more counts."
But either way,
a merry grin
is painted on my face -
for there's nothing like the feeling
of dancing with such grace.

Maja Laskowska (13)

Mirror, Mirror

Mirror, mirror, this is me,
I look at you,
And here's what I see:

There's a gap in my tooth,
And my hair's a mess,
Mirror, stop judging me,
Give it a rest!

I can be super annoying,
All my friends think I'm mad,
Mirror, shut up now,
Nobody asked!

Mirror, mirror, why can't you see?
I'm not ugly,
I'm just me!

I'm beautiful and awesome,
I don't care if you think I'm wrong,
Mirror, I'm not listening,
I've been perfect all along!

Noa Archer (13)

Georgina The Queen

I am the happiness that fills the day
But sometimes I'm the grey clouds,
Making it rain.

I am a smile,
I don't want to be a frown,
But sometimes all the stress,
Will quickly bring me down.

I want to be the story,
That somebody's going to write.
It would be all about me!
So I can be remembered all my life.

Witches, wizards, a wand and a spell,
Read a book and wish me well,
I am Georgina, crafting queen,
I'll shoot in the net
And the crowd will scream.

Georgina Stafford (11)

This Is Me

This is me
Here I am
And going far
Sprinting fast
Towards my future
This is me
Living my life
Gasping opportunities
I don't pretend to be someone else
This is me
Following my goals
My hopes
My desires
I do me and you do you
This is me
I hold firm like a rock
I don't shift
Try me
I'm anchored down
This is me
I don't give up
I don't back down
I try new things
This is me
But who are you?

Owam Makeleni (13)

I Am Growing Up

I'm growing up I think.
I'm not ready yet.
I'm not ready to leave the hazy calm days
I miss my biggest problem being a scraped knee
I miss feeling my happiest when I was swinging high
When I could count the things I was worried about on one hand.

I miss the lazy summer afternoons
Cold water fights with the garden hose.
Grass between my feet and bubbles above my head.
My chest hurting from laughter.
Fluffy pigtails and ruffled white socks.

Isabella Marsh (13)

I Want To Cry

I want to cry when my feelings are hurt,
When my eyes go red and my stomach burns,
I want to cry when I feel disappointment,
When it all goes wrong and hard work seems pointless,
I want to cry when I feel anger,
When resentment and bitterness take over,
I want to cry when my eyes start to water,
When letting it out is my best option.
But I don't want to be judged,
I don't want to look weak,
So I think it would be better,
To just keep it all in.

Leah Esson (12)

We All Fall

We all go a little insane, don't we?
In the run for our dreams, our hopes,
our delusions.
We all fall, don't we?
When we forget to watch our step, when we get pushed down,
When the weight of the world is too heavy for our shoulders.

Or when we love.

We go insane for love, don't we?
We blind ourselves to the fire and reap the warmth.
We burn our skin and believe it too feeble

We all fall, yes.
But only some are caught.

Tauheed Ali (17)

When I Run

When I run I feel alive,
All my thoughts gone, deprived.

The only thing that matters is the track ahead,
It doesn't matter what people say or have said.

My feet clawing at the tarmac,
I push and push through every setback.

I hear the beat of my heart,
Louder than cheers at the start.

When I run I learn to let things go,
Whether I'm on an all-time high or an all-time low.

I run in sun or rain,
I learn to push through the pain.

When I run I feel alive,
That is how I thrive.

Miller Webb (12)

A Whole

As a girl, I was confused about labels given to me,
A mixed child by name but whole by nature,
I am not mixed, I'm a whole,
I'm not split into quarters,
I am like everyone else - on the outside at least,
When you have parents from two different ethnicities you are called mixed...
Don't let people take away your humanity and call you that.
Labels are unnecessary,
I am me, you are you and that is the beauty of life,
Our individuality.

Harper Nayak (13)

Aren't We All The Same?

Racism does not stand by thee
And it does not make the nation for
It is discrimination

Anger fills inside me
When I hear discrimination
Any shape or size
Compared to thee

Art is different
It is a spectacle
Of beauty
Discrimination
Is a spectacle
Of exclamation

You may think discrimination
Is a joke but really
It's a joke gone too low
As low as the depths of the ocean floor.

Narayan Kolliboyana

The Truth

The truth is happiness is not always there
when you lose a close family member,
it feels like you are in the air.

The truth is happiness is our memory,
it carries us till the end,
it's like a long road showing till the end.

The truth is happiness is made for me
and this makes me very unique.

The truth is my happiness poem is coming to an end,
My name is Saima Khan and I have spoken the truth.

Saima Khan (11)

Empowered

The chains no longer hold me back,
Strands of hair in the wind flow breathtakingly.
My hands glisten glazing across the water's surface,
I take one deep breath and I feel at peace with myself,
Telling myself I can do anything
And everything,
'Reach for the stars and you will succeed'
I will take a chance at life and grab every opportunity,
I feel...
I feel...
I feel...
I am empowered.

Alana Bharucha

This Is Me

This is me, I am free.
I know who I am, I can shine.
This is me, every time.
Life can be hard sometimes, but that doesn't define who I'm meant to be.
This is me, and I will be just fine.
Things take time.
I know it with my mind, that I can drive to achieve anything I want in life.
This is me, I see it in my eyes.
I know I'm not perfect, I know I make mistakes.
But this is me, and I am free.

Cleozatra Johnson Watkis (14)

Who Am I?

Who am I
through my brother's eyes
His only friend, his therapist or his voice?

Who am I
Through my sister's eyes
Her protector, her rival or her guide

Who am I
Through my dad's eyes
His reflection, his youth or his pride

Who am I
Through my mother's eyes
Her dream come true, her last love or her life?

Who am I?

A son, a brother or a ray of light.

Azlan Khalid Noor (11)

This Is Me: I Am

Studying, trying, learning is what I do.
The only thing I see are my goals.
Yet I never physically grow.

Look around you. Take it in like I do.
Enjoying the breeze, the trees and the bees.
Life surrounds us, from the bluebell to the black bull.

The feeling of contentment when I do something fun,
Something so exhilarating like going for a run,
My adrenaline just rockets.

Nithujen Niranchan (12)

Heart And Soul

The pace of my heart
Is steady
And slow
And sometimes I wonder,
Is it beating at all?

But beyond the tall trees
And melancholy leaves
Of the mind, I will find
My old and bitter soul

And I will sit down beside it
On whatever plane it resides in
And ask it
To come out
And live in my chest.

For I am tired of diving
Down deep to find it
I am ready
To feel
Whole again.

Fiona Macmillan (14)

I Am Me

I live, I love, I cry, I lie
I have skills, I am smart
I can aim some of these darts
I can use my knowledge,
and eat some of these potato wedges.
During war, I am bruised
but my mind made me confused.
After war, I survived
except people, who cannot revive.
I continued with my life,
without any strife.
I am just... me!

Kabiven Vivekanantharajah (11)

Name

My name doesn't seem like mine sometimes,
Because I see it everywhere all of the time,
In places that hold not even a distant memory of me but of the other strangers who share this label with millions of me,
So I begin to wonder if I am it or it is me,
Because why else would I feel so detached from my name which has always belonged to just me?

Emily Schranz (16)

Reflections

I smile
He smiled back at me
Every action
Every twitch
Every whimper
Just like me
Man in the mirror
My face turned hot and his did not
My fist turned, curled and it shot
At the man in the mirror
Crying, grinning
Loving, sinning
In pieces
Just like me
Men in the mirror.

Sa'ad Adewunmi (15)

Weather

W hen it is raining it's not great
E ven inside, rain I hate
A ll the time wishing for heat
T he sun you can't beat
H ail is worse, hitting the floor the ice bursts
E ven inside, hail I hate
R ed-hot sun is better than great!

Calum Walker

This Is Me

K hloe is my name and kindness I share
H appiness is my life
L et's have a dance battle if you dare
O oh, the music makes me feel alive
E cstatic rain brings a sense of care.

Khloe Ndjoli (14)

Nothing Will Break Your Heart More

Is it better to speak or to die,
To speak is to risk,
To speak is to die,
But is it better to die and speak,
Than to die unspoken,
That is my question.

Isabella Nash (13)

YoungWriters®
Est. 1991

YOUNG WRITERS INFORMATION

We hope you have enjoyed reading this book – and that you will continue to in the coming years.

If you're the parent or family member of an enthusiastic poet or story writer, do visit our website **www.youngwriters.co.uk/subscribe** and sign up to receive news, competitions, writing challenges and tips, activities and much, much more! There's lots to keep budding writers motivated!

If you would like to order further copies of this book, or any of our other titles, then please give us a call or order via your online account.

Young Writers
Remus House
Coltsfoot Drive
Peterborough
PE2 9BF
(01733) 890066
info@youngwriters.co.uk

YoungWritersUK YoungWritersCW
youngwriterscw youngwriterscw

SCAN THE QR CODE TO WATCH THE THIS IS ME VIDEO!